GRATITUDE

GRATITUDE

10 Minutes a Day to Color Your Way

CHER KAUFMANN

The Countryman Press
A division of W. W. Norton & Company
Independent Publishers Since 1923

Copyright © 2016 by Cher Kaufmann

For information about permission to reproduce selections
from this book, write to Permissions, The Countryman Press,
500 Fifth Avenue, New York, NY 10110

For information about special discounts for bulk purchases, please
contact W. W. Norton Special Sales at specialsales@wwnorton.com
or 800-233-4830

The Countryman Press
www.countrymanpress.com

A division of W. W. Norton & Company, Inc.
500 Fifth Avenue, New York, NY 10110
www.wwnorton.com

978-1-58157-425-8 (pbk.)

10 9 8 7 6 5 4 3 2 1

To Sally, Lee and Margie, three wonderful,
amazing women who live, love,
and teach with gratitude.

INTRODUCTION

Gratitude, for some, is having nice manners and saying thank you. For others, it can mean finding peace in a moment where circumstances could be worse than they are. Gratitude is more than thank you or a sign of relief, although gratitude is felt in those situations too. Gratitude is acknowledging the harmony of giving and receiving. There are so many ways life is in constant motion: breathing, swaying, bubbling, and sailing in a sea of natural forces. There are no static moments; there is only constant motion. If life within slows down too much or stagnates in a cycle not benefiting the person, place, or object, an imbalance is created. Gratitude can help restore much of what the mind sees as serenity. Finding the harmony in giving and receiving can be healing and satisfying, and can carve a pathway to happiness.

Gratitude is accepting the good in circumstances, the gifts in wishes granted in unexpected ways, and connecting to that which has assisted in making it happen. This wonderful, sweet book on gratitude is designed to help you connect to the occasions that gift us with the harmony of giving and receiving.

How to Use this Book

- Start your day at any time—morning, afternoon, or night—with reflections from these pages.
- You may find the book helpful to read at your leisure in small, 10-minute blocks. You may reflect and contemplate the important messages any time during your day.
- You can find calm by coloring the pages provided that are paired with passages and inspirational quotes. Use this activity as a relaxing coloring meditation.
- There are lined pages with fun prompts for jotting down special memories and ideas.
- Blank pages also contain simple drawing prompts for your moments of artistic creativity.
- Randomly open to a page to see what inspiration you might gain on a given day.

*"Life is a balance of holding on
and letting go."*

—Rumi

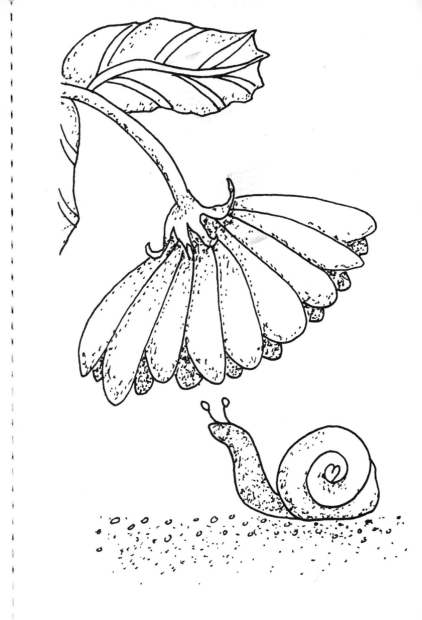

THE HUMMINGBIRD

A hummingbird was trapped in a house under construction. It kept trying to fly through the closed glass window to get outside. One of the workers saw what was happening and took his time to approach it. Eventually the bird was spent and fell to the ground. With care, the man picked it up and carried it outside, toward a tree. Weighing less than a postage stamp, the tiny creature left no physical sensations upon the man's hands. Then, gentle as a single feather barb, flew away. No evidence remains, except the memory of helping the hummingbird.

Have you had a moment no one else saw
but that was important to you?

TODAY
I AM AWARE
OF THE MANY
MOMENTS THAT
WORK IN MY
FAVOR.

See if you can find the heart in the next drawing.

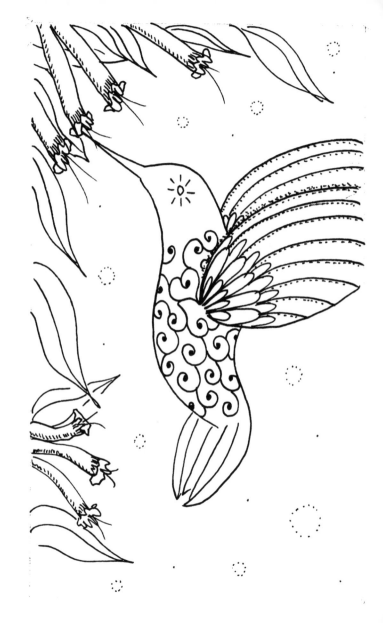

10-Minute Meditation

Conscious Breath

Sit in a comfortable position, cross-legged on the floor or upright in a chair with your feet flat, touching the earth. Sit up straight and tall. Relax your hands. Take a deep breath, allowing your shoulders to rise just ever so slightly and naturally on the inhale; then soften your shoulders—let them drop down and roll your shoulder blades closer together on the exhale. This will create a natural expansion of your chest, and open the area of the heart.

From this place of quietness, just breathe. Naturally, inward and outward. What if you allowed your body to breathe you? Let go and allow your breath to move on its own. In and out. Here, there is no "taking" of a breath—there is simply the exchange of inhale and exhale, fluidly, gently, and naturally.

Here is a moment of gratitude. You are both giving and receiving. Gratitude is harmony in giving and receiving with ease and awareness of both. Consciously giving life, consciously receiving life. Allow the corners of your mouth to gently curl upward in a soft, natural smile. Silently say "thank you" to your body and the life-giving air that have danced together in this time.

*"Gratitude is not only the greatest of virtues
but the parent of all others."*

—Cicero

Colors are often associated with certain meanings. Red=love, orange=optimism, yellow=friendship, green=newness, blue=loyalty, purple=intuition, and white=peace. If you had to put your gratitude into color, what would it look like?

Receiving the sun and the moon is natural for your body. They represent warm or cool and activity or rest. Are you most filled by the magic of sunny days or the star-lit nights between?

THE APPLE

The apple holds a secret. It contains the wisdom of the sun, acquired from many days of delightful dialogue—some warm and sunny, others cooled by the playful wind. The apple holds the gift of many rains. Soothing tales from the moon whisper in the soft cycles of waning and waxing, and the breaks of light between the leaves' shadows.

The apple has the narrative of the land, as well as the nutrients and history of all who have walked upon that land. The hands that gather apples into baskets and those who ready them for market all impart knowledge of some kind to the apple.

The apple holds more than a crisp sweetness. It possesses the secrets of the sun and the moon, the rain, the wind, the stars, and the land. All those who provided transport, including the first farmer who planted the seed, are part of the story of the apple. Each apple is a gift from the apple tree, and holds many more gifts within.

Even after all this TIME the ☀ never says to the 🌍 "YOU OWE ME." Look what happens with a ♡ like that. It 💡 up the whole sky

Sufi poet Hafiz

"Look deep into nature, and then you will understand everything better."

—Albert Einstein

In nature, plants and trees "breathe" out oxygen.
Draw and color a leaf with a smile in your heart, and a
breath of gratitude.

10-Minute Meditation

The Cliff

Imagine you are standing at the edge of a cliff. Down below, there is a large lake reflecting the deep blue of the cloudless sky. The pine trees in the distance are tall and majestic. The colors of the valley and the grass around your feet are dotted with flowers in bloom, gently swaying with a soft hello. Warmth from the sun and a soft touch from a breeze invite you to play in this glorious scene. Standing in this place, on that exact piece of ground, gives you the vista unhindered by obstacles.

Breathe in slowly, deeply. This view represents what we see when we stand in gratitude and graciousness. Each aspect is individual and important. The lake is not the tree. The bird is not the deer. Nature honors and respects each because they are all part of nature. You are also part of this nature. You have a natural place here.

Bring this in; *breathe* this in. Go forward in your day from *this* place of being.

"Just living is not enough . . . one must have sunshine, freedom, and a little flower."

—Hans Christian Andersen

TODAY I AM
APPRECIATING THE
WEATHER.
SOMEONE, SOMEWHERE
WISHES THEY COULD
TRADE PLACES WITH
ME FOR A DAY.

What is your perfect weather day?

*"To see a world in a grain of sand,
and a heaven in a wild flower,
hold infinity in the palm of your hand,
and eternity in an hour."*

—William Blake

There is evidence that pollinators are
attracted to the smell of flowers.
What aromas make you glad to be alive?

Raspberries

A large tree with a full canopy covered both our yard and part of the neighbor's yard when we first bought our house. Irises would bloom white and peach under the speckled sunlight peering through the tree's branches, but the scrawny raspberry vines produced only two raspberries in ten years. There simply was not enough sun nor bees. Because it was in an area of little traffic, we let the irises and raspberries remain under the tree without contest. One autumn afternoon, our neighbor came to our door to inform us that the tree had split in half down the center and landed in their yard. We were sad to have to cut down the broken trunk. The yard looked empty—a blank hole in the sky where the branches once held leaves, squirrels, birds, and provided shade below. Then spring arrived. The raspberries flourished. Thick green foliage, delicate white blooms, and bees—the bees!—were cross-pollinating the flowers. What a gift to have the delight of fresh raspberries.

Sometimes, when it appears something has fallen apart, it might be that its greater purpose was to bring a little sweetness into your life.

"Let gratitude be the pillow upon which you kneel to say your nightly prayer. And let faith be the bridge you build to overcome evil and welcome good."

—Maya Angelou

In every walk with Nature one receives Far MORE than he SEEKS

— John Muir —

Gratitude can be expressed in more ways than just a thank you. Sometimes a genuine smile can be a huge acknowledgment. Fill this page with smiles galore!

10-Minute Meditation

Thank You

Laughter is contagious. It lightens the energy by releasing any built-up stuckness, and also gives you a chance to really connect to humor and silliness. Laughter Yoga is a way of starting with a pretend laugh to get to a real laugh. The mind and the body don't care if you fake it—you'll receive a release of neuropeptides for pain relief and pleasure either way. Here's your chance to play.

Think of one silly time that makes you laugh (whether you experienced this in person or from a book or movie scene). Once you have the thought, laugh out loud (even if you don't feel like it at the moment). Then say "Thank you!" Think of another event that made you mad or upset and laugh out loud. Then say, "Thank you!" Repeat this five to nine times—or more if you'd like! This is really fun if you trade off sharing memories with a partner.

Remember to say "Thank you" at the end of each laugh!

TODAY
I AM SAYING
"THANK YOU"
TO ANYONE WHO
IS KIND TO
SOMEONE ELSE.

*"Gratitude is the fairest blossom
which springs from the soul."*

—Henry Ward Beecher

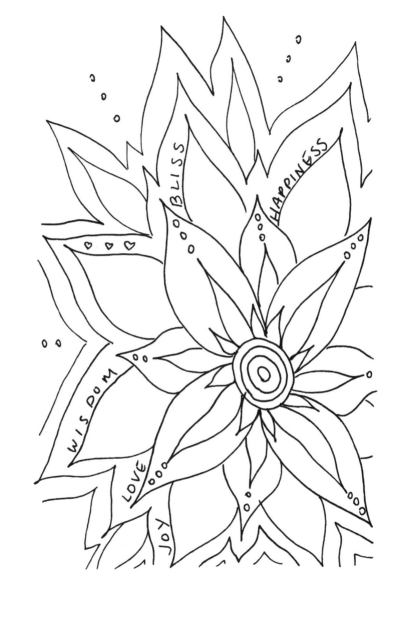

Find gratitude today. Did someone hold the door open for you? Was your morning cup of coffee piping hot? Is today a good hair day thanks to your mother's genes?

Circle your personal gratitude items on the next page.
Add more as you think of them, day by day.

I AM GRATEFUL FOR

air
music
sun
Compassion empathy travel
water happiness
Plants MOON fire
smell love
EARTH courage
trees Stars flexibility
song flexibility taste
Vision Health family
animals food language
Pets

10-Minute Meditation

Heart Smile

Master Mantak Chia shared much wisdom and knowledge in his teachings of Iron Shirt Chi Kung. One of the most important personal meditations was the Inner Smile. You can do this simple practice at any time of the day. Here is an easy way to smile to your heart.

Sit upright, erect and tall but not tightly. Sit supported on your sitz bones (the base of your pelvis). Take several deep belly breaths so the movement can massage the organs inside your abdomen. Close your eyes, relax your hands either on your knees or palms up with one palm gently resting on the other, and breathe normally. Now, imagine you are looking at your heart. See your heart with love. Smile at your heart. Smile with your lips, your mind, and your body.

Open yourself to compassion, kindness, and unconditional love. Send all these thoughts to your heart. Fill your heart with love, compassion, tenderness, and friendship. Allow your heart to feel each one of these separately and in unison. Smile and love your heart. Hold this for as long as you want. When you are ready, gently open your eyes.

"Let us be grateful to the people who make us happy; they are the charming gardeners who make our souls blossom."

—Marcel Proust

Gratitude is an attitude of allowing. Sometimes people don't realize they counter a compliment with another sentence instead of simply receiving it with a "thank you." Practice by filling the page with all kinds of "thank yous"—make them fun and creative!

TREASURE

You are a spiritual treasure. There is only one you. There is no one else exactly like you. You are a unique finger-print meant to leave your individual impression upon the world. You are here to share the richness of your being with strength and courage, vitality and wisdom. You are the sunlight that reflects upon water, shimmering with glittery shine, sending out light for others to see. Everything you behold with gentle eyes and a softened heart enlivens grati-tude and compassion in an ever-growing cycle.

When you live from a place of authenticity, you can inspire others in ways that may surprise and thrill you. Be amazed with the beauty that comes from the inner golden gem of your true nature reflecting luminescence to the world. Shine bright, little treasure, you shine much farther than your eyes can see.

List one thing you discovered about yourself in doing this exercise. (Are you grateful for your handwriting? Do you slouch or sit up when you're thinking?
Does your mind wander?)

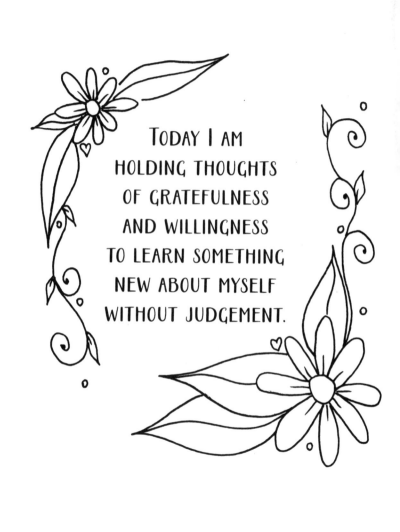

TODAY I AM
HOLDING THOUGHTS
OF GRATEFULNESS
AND WILLINGNESS
TO LEARN SOMETHING
NEW ABOUT MYSELF
WITHOUT JUDGEMENT.

*"When I let go of what I am,
I become what I might be."*

—Lao Tzu

Gratitude, by nature, opens the heart to
loving others and receiving love in return.
What's the best surprise gift you have received?

Whenever You Are SINCERELY PLEASED You Are NOURISHED

-RalphWaldoEmerson

" 'Enough' is a feast."

—Buddhist proverb

Unclutter

It can be quite challenging to appreciate what you have when you don't know what you have. In the not knowing, it is easy to move to a place of thinking where you must not have *anything* you need or want in that moment. Have you ever heard your kids or yourself say "I don't have any socks (or underwear or shorts or shoes)" simply because they were unable to see them or know where to look? In situations where that glorious missing item is found, a wave of "thank you, thank you, thank you" is fast and fleeting but happy-feeling, nonetheless.

What if you had gratitude for the items and people you DO see and use every day? What if you uncluttered the mess and put the laundry away? Imagine the ease and smoothness a day could begin and end with if you had access to all you needed, and it wasn't hidden anywhere.

Create harmony between yourself and your environment by cleaning three things out of your closet. Draw what harmony looks like to you.